The Christmas Story

Joseph, Mary, and the Baby Jesus From a Personal Perspective

Randal S. Chase

Edited by Michael D. Chase

The Christmas Story:
Joseph, Mary, and the Baby Jesus From a Personal Perspective

Send inquiries to:
Plain and Precious Publishing
3378 E. Sweetwater Springs Drive
Washington, UT 84780

Send e-mail: info@makingpreciousthingsplain.com

For more copies visit www.makingpreciousthingsplain.com

For a listing of all Plain and Precious Publishing products,
visit www.makingpreciousthingsplain.com
or call 435–251–8520.

Printed in the United States of America

ISBN: 978-1-937901-00-4

Cover: "Journey to Bethlehem" by Joseph Brickey ©. Used by Permission.

The Christmas Story:

Joseph, Mary, and the Baby Jesus From a Personal Perspective

Table of Contents

J. AUBERT, THE BIBLE AND ITS STORY, 1908

Joseph, Mary, and the Baby Jesus

Chapter 1

Introduction

(Luke 2; 1 Nephi 11)

A Family Story

The story of the birth of Jesus is a family story: the story of a father, a mother, and the birth of their very first child. The tenderness of this story still touches and inspires us after many centuries. In this book we will tell the story once again, but this time by examining the individuals within it—John the Baptist, Nephi, Joseph, Mary, and the baby Jesus—as the extraordinary people who played a major role in the nativity of our Lord Jesus Christ.

We glean most of what we know about this story from three sources: Luke 2 tells us the tender story of the women, of cousins, of babies, of angels, and of shepherds. Matthew tells us the story of Joseph and of his genealogy. And the Book of Mormon tells of the prophecies that predicted Jesus's birth years before it occurred. We will draw on all three of these accounts in our attempt to understand the entire story in context.

The Decree of Caesar Augustus

¶ Luke 2:1–3

Caesar Augustus ordered a general taxing (census) of the Roman Empire in 1 B.C.

We can set the date by virtue of the fact that it began when "Cyrenius was governor of Syria" (v. 2). In the land of Israel, people traveled to their city of origin to be taxed (v. 3).

Elder James E. Talmage said: "The taxing herein referred to may properly be understood as an enrollment, or a registration, whereby a census of Roman subjects would be secured, upon which as a basis the taxation of the different peoples would be determined. . . . Had the census been taken by the usual Roman method, each person would have been enrolled at the town of his residence; but the Jewish custom, for which the Roman law had respect, necessitated registration at the cities or towns claimed by the respective families as their ancestral homes."[1]

The Date of Christ's Birth

Elder Bruce R. McConkie said: "From the first sentence of the revelation given to Joseph Smith on the day the Church was organized in this dispensation [D&C 20:1], it appears that the latter-day kingdom formally came into being on the eighteen hundred and thirtieth anniversary of our Lord's birth. In other words, Christ was born April 6, B.C. 1."[2] The following chart helps to visualize the date of His birth:

The Condescension of God

¶ 1 Nephi 11:14–18, 20–21

Nephi learns that the Savior's birth is a demonstration of the "condescension" of God.

Nephi had asked what the tree of life stood for, and in response, "an angel came down and stood before [him]; and he said unto [him]: Nephi, what beholdest thou?" (v. 14). He was seeing a vision of the Virgin Mary. He answered, "A virgin, most beautiful and fair above all other virgins" (v. 15). And the angel then asked, "Knowest thou the condescension of God?" (v. 16).

W. A. BOUGUEREAU, 1893

Nephi saw Mary holding the Baby Jesus in her arms

The angel's question is a good one: Do we understand the "condescension" of Christ's birth? To condescend means to lower oneself to the level of another person. The God Jehovah was condescending Himself when He became a mortal in order to save us. Nephi needed to understand this in order to understand the birth of Christ.

Nephi said to the angel, "I know that he [God] loveth his children; nevertheless, I do not know the meaning of all things" (v. 17). And the angel continued his explanation by saying, "The virgin whom thou seest is the mother of the Son of God, after the manner of the flesh" (v. 18). "And I looked and beheld the virgin again, bearing a child in her arms. And the angel said unto me: Behold the Lamb of God, yea, even the Son of the Eternal Father!" (vv. 20–21).

The tree of life represents what Nephi was then gazing upon: the mortal advent of the Son of God. This supernal act of love on His part makes our salvation and exaltation possible. Thus, the tree represents the love of God—His willingness to condescend from His throne on high in order to save us. The greatest of all the children of God—His eldest Son—the Creator of all things throughout the universe—was born in a filthy stable—wrapped in rags—virtually unnoticed by the world He came to save.

Notes

1. *Jesus the Christ*, 3rd ed. (1916), 91–92.
2. *Doctrinal New Testament Commentary*, 3 vols. (1965–73), 1:91.

Chapter 2

John the Baptist

(Luke 1; Matthew 23)

John the Baptist's Birth Announced

¶ Luke 1:5–17

Gabriel announces John the Baptist's birth to his father Zacharias.

In the days of Herod the king of Judea, the temple priests took turns officiating in "courses." Zacharias was one of those priests. At the time of this visitation, his course (Abia) was officiating (v. 5), and it was Zacharias's duty to keep the altar of incense burning in the Holy Place of the Temple (vv. 8–9).

His wife, Elisabeth, was also a descendant of Aaron, and they were both righteous, "walking in all the commandments and ordinances of the Lord blameless" (v. 6). Zacharias and Elisabeth were childless and "well stricken in years" (v. 7), having sought the Lord in prayer for many years that they might be blessed with posterity.

On this particular day, "the whole multitude of the people were praying" outside the temple at the time when Zacharias went in to burn the incense (v. 10). While there, an angel of the Lord appeared to Zacharias, "standing on the right side of the altar of incense" (v. 11). We learn a few verses later that this angel was Gabriel (v. 19), who, as we know from modern revelation, is Noah.[1]

Zacharias was surprised by this appearance, "and fear fell upon him" (v. 12). "But the angel said unto him, Fear not, Zacharias: for thy prayer is heard; and thy wife Elisabeth shall bear thee a son, and

Gabriel appeared to Zacharias in the temple

thou shalt call his name John. And thou shalt have joy and gladness; and many shall rejoice at his birth" (vv. 13–14).

This was reason enough to rejoice, but there was more. The angel said: "He shall be great in the sight of the Lord, and shall drink neither wine nor strong drink [meaning he would be a Nazarite]; and he shall be filled with the Holy Ghost, even from his mother's womb" (v. 15). He would be a prophet whose mission would be to turn the children of Israel toward the Lord (v. 16). He would possess "the spirit and power of Elias, to turn the hearts of the fathers to the children, and the disobedient to the wisdom of the just; to make ready a people prepared for the Lord" (v. 17). Thus, he would be the promised Elias who would prepare the way for the coming of the Lord to earth (Isaiah 40:3).

❡ Luke 1:18–23
Zacharias is struck dumb.

Zacharias was incredulous. "Whereby shall I know this?" he asked, "for I am an old man, and my wife well stricken in years" (v. 18). This manifestation of doubt was certainly understandable by earthly standards, but he was speaking to an angel sent from the presence of God (v. 19). Thus, the sign he was granted was also a punishment.

Zacharias was struck dumb

"Behold, thou shalt be dumb, and not able to speak, until the day that these things shall be performed, because thou believest not my words, which shall be fulfilled in their season" (v. 20). And then the vision closed.

Meanwhile, outside the temple, the people were wondering why he took so long to perform the simple task of refreshing the altar of incense (v. 21). When he finally came out, "he could not speak unto them: and they perceived that he had seen a vision in the temple" (v. 22). He beckoned unto them, but remained speechless. This malady continued for the rest of the days of his assignment at the temple, and even afterward when he returned home (v. 23).

❡ Luke 1:24–25
Elisabeth conceives a son.

Very soon after this, "Elisabeth conceived, and hid herself five months" (v. 24). She rejoiced at this great miracle, saying,

"Thus hath the Lord dealt with me in the days wherein he looked on me, to take away my reproach among men" (v. 25).

C. H. BLOCH, 1860s

Mary visited her cousin Elisabeth

¶ Luke 1:26–27
Gabriel's annunciation to Mary.

Luke breaks off from his narrative of John the Baptist's birth to tell us that "in the sixth month [of Elisabeth's pregnancy] the angel Gabriel was sent from God unto a city of Galilee, named Nazareth, to a virgin espoused to a man whose name was Joseph, of the house of David; and the virgin's name was Mary" (vv. 26–27). This is how we know that John the Baptist was six months older than the Savior.

Mary Visits Elisabeth

¶ Luke 1:39–40
Mary visits her cousin Elisabeth.

After hearing of her heavenly assignment and conceiving the Christ child, "Mary arose . . . and went into the hill country with haste, into a city of Juda; And entered into the house of Zacharias, and saluted Elisabeth" (vv. 39–40).

This was an ideal arrangement. Elisabeth could provide family support to Mary in a location where her pregnancy would not raise continual questions from those around her. At the same time, Mary, who was early in her pregnancy, could provide help to Elisabeth, who was in the later stages of her own pregnancy. They could help each other.

¶ Luke 1:41–45
Elisabeth and her unborn baby recognize the mother of our Lord.

No sooner did Mary greet Elisabeth than "the babe leaped in her womb; and Elisabeth was filled with the Holy Ghost" (v. 41). Elisabeth loudly proclaimed her great admiration for Mary and her unborn child. "Blessed art thou among women, and blessed is the fruit of thy womb," she said (v. 42). How could it be, she wondered, that "the mother of my Lord should come to me?" (v. 43). "For, lo, as soon as the voice of thy salutation sounded in mine ears, the babe leaped in my womb for joy" (v. 44).

She reassured Mary that, because of her faith, "there shall be a performance of those things which were told her from the Lord" (v. 45). Mary's response to Elisabeth's greeting is discussed in chapter 4.

¶ Luke 1:56

Mary stays until John is born.

The scripture records that "Mary abode with her about three months, and returned to her own house." That would have been the last three months of Elisabeth's pregnancy, since she arrived when Elisabeth was in her sixth month. And since this was in Mary's third month of pregnancy, it follows that John the Baptist was born just six months earlier than Jesus.

The Birth of John the Baptist

¶ Luke 1:57–58

John the Baptist is born.

When Elisabeth arrived at her full term of pregnancy, "she brought forth a son" as the angel had promised she would (v. 57). Her family and friends rejoiced at this miraculous birth (v. 58), one that would never have been imagined possible for a woman of Elisabeth's age. Elisabeth's child was John the Baptist—a second cousin to Jesus, since Mary and Elisabeth were first cousins

¶ Luke 1:59–64

Obedient to Gabriel, Zacharias names his son John.

Obedient to the law, "on the eighth day they came to circumcise the child; and they called him Zacharias, after the name of his father" (v. 59). But Elisabeth corrected them. "Not so; but he shall be called John" (v. 60).

This was unusual, because there was nobody among her immediate kindred who had this name (v. 61). They appealed to Zacharias concerning the matter and asked what name he would give the child (v. 62). Being unable to speak, "he asked for a writing table, and wrote, saying, His name is John" (v. 63). And immediately "his mouth was opened . . . and his tongue loosed, and he spake, and praised God" (v. 64).

J. S. V. CAROLSFELD, 1852-1860

¶ Luke 1:80
Jesus and John the Baptist were of similar age.

The scriptures say of John, "The child grew, and waxed strong in spirit." As a young boy, he certainly must have visited and known Jesus, being only six months older than He. Also, his parents Zacharias and Elisabeth lived near Jerusalem.

¶ Matthew 23:34–36
Jesus alludes to Zacharias's murder.

As the Lord Jehovah, He had sent prophets unto Judah (including Himself) only to have them killed and crucified, "scourge[d] in [their] synagogues, and persecute[d] . . . from city to city" (v. 34). These murderous acts would bring upon them "all the righteous blood shed upon the earth, from the blood of righteous Abel unto

RUBENS, 1616

Jesus and John the Baptist were of similar age

the blood of Zacharias . . . whom [they] slew between the temple and the altar" (v. 35).

JAMES J. TISSOT, 1904

The Prophet Joseph Smith said: "When Herod's edict went forth to destroy the young children, John was about six months older than Jesus, and came under this hellish edict, and Zacharias caused [John's] mother to take him into the mountains, where he was raised on locusts and wild honey. When his father refused to disclose his hiding place, and being the officiating high priest at the Temple that year, was slain by Herod's order, between the porch and the altar, as Jesus said."[2]

¶ Luke 1:80

John the Baptist grew safely to manhood.

Having been protected in his wilderness hiding place, John the Baptist "grew, and waxed strong in spirit, and was in the deserts till the day of his shewing unto Israel."

Elder Bruce R. McConkie said:

> As is the case with his kinsman Jesus, the scriptures are virtually silent on the life and labors of John prior to his formal ministry, which commenced, according to Levitical law, when he was thirty years of age (Num. 4:3, 47). We do know that "he was baptized while he was yet in his childhood" (D&C 84:28), meaning when he was eight years of age; that his parents were faithful and righteous people; that he "was a priest after his father, and held the keys of the Aaronic priesthood, and was called of God to preach the Gospel of the kingdom of God;"[3] that he "waxed strong in spirit," that is, became a tower of spiritual strength; and that he was guided during his whole life by the Holy Ghost. It naturally follows that he was trained in obedience to the law of Moses, officiated in the Levitical ordinances and performances, was married (an almost mandatory social requirement among the Jews), and probably had children.[4]

Notes

1. See *History of the Church*, 3:386.
2. "Persecution of the Prophets," *Times and Seasons*, Sept. 1, 1842, 902.
3. *History of the Church*, 5:257.
4. *Doctrinal New Testament Commentary*, 3 vols. (1965–73), 1:89–90.

Chapter 3

Joseph the Carpenter

(Luke 1; Matthew 1)

The Importance of Joseph's Role

Though he is sometimes the "forgotten person" of Jesus's nativity, Joseph was, without a doubt, an essential part of Jesus's birth and upbringing. His love for Mary is evident in his mercy upon learning of her pregnancy, and in his loving care thereafter as he sought in vain to find her some comfort when the day of the baby's birth arrived.

As a man, he courageously provided for and protected Jesus's life, taking Him into Egypt for a time to avoid the murderous plots of Herod. He was the earthly guardian of Christ, treating Him as his own son in every respect, teaching Him from the scriptures, and teaching Him the craft of carpentry to sustain Him in His early manhood. Thus, Joseph was the role model for Christ in both temporal and spiritual things.

RAPHAEL, 1506

Joseph, Mary, and the baby Jesus

Joseph was also the father of a later Apostle—James, the brother of the Lord, who wrote the book of

James in our Bible. And he was the father of Jude—not an Apostle but an inspired leader and writer who wrote the book of Jude in our Bible.

Legend suggests that Joseph did not survive to the time of Jesus's ministry. We do not hear of him in the scriptures after the time of the Savior's youth. He may have been older than Mary. But they clearly loved each other and are eternal companions now.

Joseph remains, for me and for others, a hero—a man who did not react with macho anger or abuse but rather gentle forgiveness when he learned of Mary's plight. His faith, his loyalty, his willingness to play the role of earthly father to the Son of God—all of these bear witness that he was a chosen man in God's plan for the birth and childhood of His Son.

The Genealogy of Joseph

¶ Matthew 1:1–17; Luke 3:23–28
Jesus descended from kings.

There are two genealogies in the Gospels. Matthew's account lists the legal successors to David's throne. This was not a strict father-to-son genealogy because the eldest surviving heir at any point along the line may have been a grandson, a great-grandson, a nephew, or another relative of the previous king.

Luke's record, however, is a father-to-son listing of kings which eventually terminates with Jesus through Mary. Of course, Jesus was not Joseph's literal son, but Joseph's genealogy is essentially the same as Mary's because they were cousins. Thus, Jesus inherited from His mother, Mary, the blood of David and from His "father" Joseph the official royal line. Either way, Jesus had the right to David's throne.

Elder James E. Talmage said: "Had Judah been a free and independent nation, ruled by her rightful sovereign, Joseph the carpenter would have been her crowned king; and his lawful successor to the throne would have been Jesus of Nazareth, the King of the Jews."[1]

Mary and Joseph Were Espoused

As the story begins, Joseph and Mary were not yet married, but were promised to each other under the strictest terms. During espousal, Mary was regarded as virtually the wife of Joseph. A woman and her espoused husband were strictly separated and never allowed to communicate directly, so any kind of direct contact with Joseph would have been inappropriate. During the espousal period, the bride-elect lived with her family or friends and all communication with her promised husband was carried on through a friend. Of course, any contact with another man would have also been inappropriate, and any kind of unfaithfulness during espousal was punishable by death. It was during the time of their espousal that Joseph learned of Mary's pregnancy.

Joseph Was "A Just Man"

¶ Matthew 1:18
The shocking news comes to Joseph.

"Now the birth of Jesus Christ was on this wise: When as his mother Mary was espoused to Joseph, before they came together, she was found with child of the Holy Ghost."

We can only imagine the agony and torment of uncertainty and doubt that must have filled the soul of Joseph. He knew for certain that he was not the father. He could not talk to Mary directly to hear her side of the story. He had received no heavenly vision to tell him otherwise, so he had to assume that Mary had been unfaithful to him. He could have reacted selfishly and with bitterness, and if he did, who could blame him? All his hopes and plans now seemed dashed.

When Joseph learned of Mary's maternity, he had two alternatives under the law:

—Require that Mary submit to a public trial and judgment, resulting in her death, or . . .

—Privately sever the espousal contract before witnesses.

JAMES J. TISSOT, 1904

Initially, Joseph did not understand what was happening

¶ Matthew 1:19

Joseph's love and mercy for Mary.

"Then Joseph her husband, being a just man, and not willing to make her a publick example, was minded to put her away privily." Despite his agony, Joseph chose the more merciful of the two alternatives, which reveals much about his character.

Elder James E. Talmage said: "Joseph was a just man, a strict observer of the law, yet no harsh extremist; moreover he loved Mary and would save her all unnecessary humiliation, whatever might be his own sorrow and suffering. For Mary's sake he dreaded the thought of publicity; and therefore determined to have the espousal annulled with such privacy as the law allowed."[2]

Gabriel Appears to Joseph

¶ Matthew 1:20–21

The Angel Gabriel appears and explains everything to Joseph.

"While he [Joseph] thought on these things, behold, the angel of the Lord appeared unto him in a dream, saying, Joseph, thou son of David, fear not to take unto thee Mary thy wife: for that which is conceived in her is of the Holy Ghost. And she shall bring forth a son, and thou shalt call his name Jesus: for he shall save his people from their sins" (vv. 20–21).

Notice that it was after his trial of faith that the angel came to explain it all. Joseph's mercy for Mary was shown without fully understanding what was happening to her. But after he made his merciful choice, the angel came and explained it all to him.

¶ Matthew 1:24–25

Joseph obeys immediately.

"Then Joseph being raised from sleep did as the angel of the Lord had bidden him, and took unto him his wife" (v. 24). The consummation of their marriage would have to wait. Joseph "knew her not" until after she had given birth to the baby Jesus (v. 25). But he became her husband and protector immediately.

CARL HEINRICH BLOCH, 1875

Joseph Takes Mary and Jesus into Egypt

Within two years of the birth of Jesus, the wise men came from the east to worship Him. When King Herod asked why they had come, and they made mention of a newborn king, he did not intend to allow a rival king to survive. After carefully determining where the child was prophesied to be born, he plotted to assassinate the Christ child (Matthew 2:4–7).

¶ Matthew 2:13–15
Joseph and Mary flee into Egypt with the baby.

An angel of the Lord "appear[ed] to Joseph in a dream, saying, Arise, and take the young child and his mother, and flee into Egypt, and be thou there until I bring thee word: for Herod will seek the young child to destroy him" (v. 13). And "when he arose, he took the young child and his mother by night, and departed into Egypt" (v. 14), where the young family remained "until the death of Herod" (v. 15).

¶ Matthew 2:15
"Out of Egypt have I called my Son."

There were many prophecies concerning the place from which the Messiah would come. One predicted the area surrounding Nazareth (Isaiah 9:1) and another the city of Bethlehem (Micah 5:2). A third said that he would come out of Egypt (Hosea 11:1). In the end, all three turned out to be correct, and this sojourn into Egypt provided the circumstances under which Hosea's prophecy was fulfilled.

Matthew 2:1	He was born in Bethlehem Fulfillment of Micah 5:2
Matthew 2:23	He was raised in Nazareth Fulfillment of Isaiah 9:1
Matthew 2:15	He came out of Egypt Fulfillment of Hosea 11:1

C. H. BLOCK

¶ Matthew 2:16–18

Herod slaughters all children in Bethlehem under two years old.

When the wise men failed to return, Herod "was exceeding wroth, and sent forth, and slew all the children that were in Bethlehem, and in all the coasts thereof, from two years old and under" (v. 16).

This was based on the information given him from the wise men concerning when the star first appeared in the sky. We can deduce, then, that Jesus was around two years of age when the wise men visited Him. This bloody slaughter of innocent children also fulfilled prophecy. Jeremiah had predicted "a [great] voice [of] lamentation" in Ramah, "and weeping, and great mourning, Rachel weeping for her children, and would not be comforted, because they are not" (vv. 17–18; Jeremiah 31:15).

Elder James E. Talmage said: "Herod was professedly an adherent of the religion of Judah, though by birth an Idumean, by descent an Edomite or one of the posterity of Esau, all of whom the Jews hated; and of all Edomites not one was more bitterly detested than was Herod the king. He was tyrannical and merciless, sparing neither foe nor friend who came under suspicion of being a possible hindrance to his ambitious designs. He had his wife and several of his sons, as well as others of his blood kindred, cruelly murdered; and he put to death nearly all of the great national council, the Sanhedrin. His reign was one of revolting cruelty and unbridled oppression. Only when in danger of inciting a national revolt or in fear of incurring the displeasure of his imperial master, the Roman emperor, did he stay his hand in any undertaking."[3]

¶ Matthew 2:19–23

Joseph, Mary, and the baby return to Nazareth.

When Herod died (estimated to be within two more years), "an angel of the Lord appear[ed] in a dream to Joseph in Egypt, saying, Arise, and take the young child and his mother, and go into the land of Israel: for they are dead which sought the young child's life" (vv. 19–20).

Obediently, "he arose, and took the young child and his mother, and came into the land of Israel" (v. 21). He was warned in a dream that it was not safe to return to Judea, where Herod's son Archelaus now reigned, so "he turned aside into the parts of Galilee" and "came and dwelt in a city called Nazareth: that it might be fulfilled which was spoken by the prophets, He shall be called a Nazarene" (vv. 22–23).

A. BIDA, 1874

Notes

1. *Jesus the Christ*, 3rd ed. (1916), 87.
2. *Jesus the Christ*, 84.
3. *Jesus the Christ*, 97–98.

RUBENS, 1628

Mary: A chosen daughter of God

Chapter 4

Mary the Mother of God

(Luke 1; Matthew 1)

A Special Daughter of God

Mary's role was truly prophetic. Isaiah spoke of her 700 years earlier when he prophesied, "Behold, a virgin shall conceive, and bear a son, and shall call his name Immanuel" (Isaiah 7:14). Nephi called her "a virgin, most beautiful and fair above all other virgins" (1 Nephi 11:15). King Benjamin knew that the mother of God would be named Mary (Mosiah 3:8), and Alma called her "a precious and chosen vessel" (Alma 7:10).

Mary came from a small and inconsequential village called Nazareth. It was so little regarded that when Nathanael heard Philip say that Jesus was the Christ, he commented, "Can there any good thing come out of Nazareth?" (John 1:46). We answer, "Yes, Mary did. And she was the mother of our God."

Elder Bruce R. McConkie said: "Can we speak too highly of her whom the Lord has blessed above all women? There was only one Christ, and there is only one Mary. . . . We cannot but think that the Father would choose the greatest female spirit to be the mother of His Son."[1]

Elder McConkie also said: "As the Father chose the most noble and righteous of all His spirit sons to come into mortality as His Only Begotten in the flesh, so we may confidently conclude that

He selected the most worthy and spiritually talented of all His spirit daughters to be the mortal mother of His Eternal Son."[2]

Mary Learns of Her Sacred Mission

¶ Luke 1:26–30

Gabriel's annunciation to Mary.

It was during "the sixth month [of Elisabeth's pregnancy that] the angel Gabriel was sent from God unto a city of Galilee, named Nazareth, to a virgin espoused to a man whose name was Joseph, of the house of David; and the virgin's name was Mary" (vv. 26–27). This is how we know that John the Baptist was six months older than the Savior.

The Prophet Joseph Smith tells us that Gabriel is Noah.[3] This ancient prophet—the father of us all—had already annunciated John the Baptist's birth to his father Zacharias. Now, he appeared to the young virgin Mary, saying, "Hail, thou that art highly favoured, the Lord is with thee: blessed art thou among women" (v. 28). This was an odd salutation, and the young girl was somewhat troubled by its praise (v. 29). Gabriel noticed and reassured her: "Fear not, Mary: for thou hast found favour with God" (v. 30).

¶ Luke 1:31–35

Mary learns that she will be the mother of the Son of God.

Gabriel told her that "thou shalt conceive in thy womb, and bring forth a son, and shalt call his name Jesus" (v. 31). "He shall be great, and shall be called the Son of the Highest" (v. 32). This was very surprising news to a young virgin who was not yet married—only espoused. "How shall this be," she asked, "seeing I know not [have never had intercourse with] a man?" (v. 34). "And the angel answered and said unto her, The Holy Ghost shall come upon thee, and the power of the Highest shall overshadow thee: therefore also that holy thing which shall be born of thee shall be called the Son of God" (v. 35). Thus, the baby's father would be God the Father Himself and Mary would be His earthly mother. Moreover, "the Lord God shall give unto him the throne of his father David: And he

C. H. BLOCH, 1875

Gabriel's annunciation to Mary

shall reign over the house of Jacob or ever; and of his kingdom there shall be no end" (vv. 32–33). She would be the mother of the King of Kings.

At this news, Mary certainly must have been overwhelmed. According to legend, she was only about 16 years old, had never been married, and had never had a child. Her conception would be miraculous and unique. God the Eternal Father would be the father of her child. Yet, even after conception, she would remain a virgin. It had never happened before, and would never happen again, worlds without end.

¶ WHO WOULD BELIEVE HER EXPLANATION?
She must have had many concerns as she tried to absorb this heavenly message.

—Would Joseph believe her? She could not explain things to him face to face.
—Would her family believe her? Or would they simply cast her out?
—Would anybody else believe her? Some did not. They said that Christ was "born of fornication" (John 8:41).
—Even today, many Christians, including pastors, do not believe in the virgin birth. We are left to wonder: "Just whose child do they think Jesus was? A child of fornication?"

¶ Luke 1:38
Mary humbly accepted her assignment with faith.

Despite these concerns, Mary said simply to the angel: "Behold the handmaid of the Lord; be it unto me according to thy word. And the angel departed from her."

False Doctrines About Mary Abound

Heresy #1: A persistent heresy, particularly in the Church, is that God the Father must have had sexual intercourse with Mary. There is nothing whatsoever in the scriptures to support this notion. We are told that she was "overshadowed" by the Holy Ghost and that through that Spirit's instrumentality the conception occurred

(Alma 7:10). And we are specifically told by Isaiah that a virgin would conceive (Isaiah 7:14). She was a virgin before the conception and a virgin afterwards. And I think, sometimes, that those who insist otherwise might be doing so in order to shock and to wrest the scriptures to their own provocative notions.

I am perfectly aware of the statement of Elder Bruce R. McConkie on this topic that says that Jesus was conceived in the same manner as all babies are conceived. But let us carefully consider what he actually said:

Elder Bruce R. McConkie said:

> [Gabriel was] telling her in plain words the status and mission and dominion of Him who was to be her Son: "He shall be great, and shall be called the Son of the Highest: and the Lord God shall give unto him the throne of his father David: And he shall reign over the house of Jacob for ever; and of his kingdom there shall be no end."
>
> "The Son of the Highest"—the Supreme God shall be His Father! "The throne of his father David"—the symbol of all Jewish hope and triumph and glory and freedom and deliverance! An eternal kingdom—the kingdom of our God and of His Christ, and they shall reign forever and ever!
>
> Mary asked, "How shall this be, seeing I know not a man?" Obviously she could, at the proper time, know Joseph, and he could be the father of all her children, not just those who would come after the Firstborn. She knew that. But already the concept was framed in her mind that the promised Son was not to originate from any power on earth.
>
> This offspring was to be Himself almighty—God's Almighty Son. How and by what means and through whose instrumentality does such a conception come?
>
> Gabriel explains: "The Holy Ghost shall come upon thee, and the power of the Highest shall overshadow thee: therefore also that holy thing [better, that holy child] which shall be born of thee shall be called the Son of God."
>
> Again the answer is perfect. There is a power beyond man's. When God is involved, He uses His minister, the Holy Ghost, to overshadow the future mother and to carry her away in the Spirit. She shall conceive by the power of the Holy Ghost, and God Himself shall be the sire. It is His Son of whom Gabriel is speaking. A son is begotten by a father: whether on earth or in heaven it is the same.[4]

But we are not justified in jumping from that statement—that God the Father was the sire whose seed mixed with Mary's to produce the holy child—to a claim that intercourse between God the Father and Mary was necessary. Ask any childless couple in the world and they will tell you that there is not necessarily a connection between copulation and conception—either one can occur without the other. Conception occurs when the seed of a man and the seed of a woman are joined to form a new life. Let us not attempt to bring God "down to our level" by insisting that He could not have produced conception without intercourse. Neither science nor common sense support such a claim.

The conception of Mary's child was miraculous and unique. It had never happened before, and it will never happen again. It was a once-in-the-universe epochal event:

— God the Father was the father. Luke 1:32 says Jesus was the "Son of the Highest."

— Mary remained a virgin. Isaiah 7:14 says "a virgin shall conceive."

— Never before and never again. D&C 76:23 says Jesus is "the Only Begotten of the Father."

Heresy #2: A second heresy, found both within the Church and among some Christians generally, is that the Holy Ghost was the father of Jesus.

Elder Bruce R. McConkie said:

> Apostate religionists—unable to distinguish between the Father, Son, and Holy Ghost—falsely suppose that the Holy Ghost was the Father of our Lord. Matthew's statement, "she was found with child of the Holy Ghost," properly translated should say, *'she was found with child by the power of the Holy Ghost'* (Matt. 1:18). Luke's account (Luke 1:35) accurately records what took place. Alma perfectly describes our Lord's conception and birth by prophesying: Christ "shall be born of Mary, . . . she being a virgin, a precious and chosen vessel, who shall be overshadowed and *conceive by the power of the Holy Ghost*, and bring forth a son, yea, even *the Son of God*" [Alma 7:10; italics added]. Nephi spoke similarly when he said that at the time of her conception, Mary "was carried away in the Spirit," with the

result that the child born of her was "the Lamb of God, yea, even the Son of the Eternal Father" (1 Ne. 11:19–21). As Gabriel [said], He was the "Son of the Highest" (Luke 1:32), and "the Highest" is the first member of the godhead, not the third.[5]

Heresy #3: A third heresy is one put forward by early and uninspired Christian councils and sectarians. They say that Mary was indeed a virgin after she conceived and that she remained a virgin forever thereafter. Daniel H. Ludlow said: "The promise that the mother of Jesus would be 'a virgin' at the time of the birth of Jesus should *not* be interpreted to mean that she would remain a virgin throughout her life. The false doctrine of the 'perpetual virginity' of Mary is not substantiated from the scriptures. Indeed, 'brothers and sisters' of Jesus are specifically mentioned later in the record" [Matt. 12:46–50; Mark 3:31–35; Luke 8:19–21].[6]

Jesus Was Both Mortal and Immortal

To accomplish His mission, Jesus had to have both mortal and immortal parents.

Elder Bruce R. McConkie said:

> God was His Father, from which Immortal Personage . . . He inherited the power of immortality, which is the power to live forever; or, having chosen to die, it is the power to rise again in immortality, thereafter to live forever without again seeing corruption. . . .
>
> Mary was His mother, from which mortal woman . . . He inherited the power of mortality, which is the power to die. . . .
>
> It was because of this . . . intermixture of the divine and the mortal in one person, that our Lord was able to work out the infinite and eternal atonement. Because God was His Father and Mary was His mother, He had power to live or to die, as He chose, and having laid down His life, He had power to take it again, and then, in a way incomprehensible to us, to pass on the effects of that resurrection to all men so that all shall rise from the tomb.[7]

Elder James E. Talmage said: "That Child to be born of Mary was begotten of Elohim, the Eternal Father, not in violation of natural law but in accordance with a higher manifestation thereof;

and, the offspring from that association of supreme sanctity, celestial Sireship, and pure though mortal maternity, was of right to be called the 'Son of the Highest.' In His nature would be combined the powers of Godhood with the capacity and possibilities of mortality; and this through the ordinary operation of the fundamental law of heredity, declared of God, demonstrated by science, and admitted by philosophy, that living beings shall propagate—after their kind. The Child Jesus was to inherit the physical, mental, and spiritual traits, tendencies, and powers that characterized His parents—one immortal and glorified—God, the other human—woman."[8]

Mary Is Sheltered by Elisabeth

Happily, we learn that Mary's family did believe and support her. Joseph immediately married her, as instructed by the angel Gabriel. And her cousin Elisabeth sheltered her.

¶ Luke 1:39–40
Mary visits her cousin Elisabeth.

After hearing of her heavenly assignment and conceiving the Christ child, "Mary arose . . . and went into the hill country with haste, into a city of Juda; And entered into the house of Zacharias, and saluted Elisabeth" (vv. 39–40).

This was an ideal arrangement. Elisabeth could provide family support to Mary in a location where her pregnancy would not raise continual questions from those around her. At the same

C. H. BLOCH, 1860s

time, Mary, who was early in her pregnancy, could provide help to Elisabeth, who was in the later stages of her own pregnancy. They could help each other.

¶ Luke 1:41–45
Elisabeth and her unborn baby recognize the mother of our Lord.

No sooner did Mary greet Elisabeth than "the babe leaped in her womb; and Elisabeth was filled with the Holy Ghost" (v. 41). Elisabeth loudly proclaimed her great admiration for Mary and her unborn child. "Blessed art thou among women, and blessed is the fruit of thy womb," she said (v. 42). How could it be, she wondered, that "the mother of my Lord should come to me?" (v. 43). "For, lo, as soon as the voice of thy salutation sounded in mine ears, the babe leaped in my womb for joy" (v. 44). She reassured Mary that, because of her faith, "there shall be a performance of those things which were told her from the Lord" (v. 45).

¶ Luke 1:41, 44
When does the spirit enter the body of an unborn child?

Elder Bruce R. McConkie said: "In this miraculous event the pattern is seen which a spirit follows in passing from his pre-existent first estate into mortality. The spirit enters the body at the time of quickening, months prior to the actual normal birth. The value and comfort attending a knowledge of this eternal truth is seen in connection with stillborn children. Since the spirit entered the body before birth, stillborn children will be resurrected and righteous parents shall enjoy their association in immortal glory."[9]

¶ Luke 1:46–55
Mary's prophetic response.

Mary's response to Elisabeth's salutation was both humble and prophetic. "My soul doth magnify the Lord," she said, "and my spirit hath rejoiced in God my Saviour. For he hath regarded the low estate of his handmaiden" (vv. 46–48). That was the humble part, and it reveals that she did not think she was any more righteous or deserving than other women by virtue of this assignment.

Nevertheless, she recognized the greatness of her calling. "From henceforth all generations shall call me blessed," she said, "for he that is mighty hath done to me great things; and holy is his name" (vv. 48–49). She knew that God the Father had fathered her child and it was an eternally unique blessing to have been a partner with Him in providing an earthly tabernacle for the Savior of the world.

Speaking of our Father in Heaven, she said: "His mercy is on them that fear him from generation to generation. He hath shewed strength with his arm; he hath scattered the proud in the imagination of their hearts. He hath put down the mighty from their seats, and exalted them of low degree. He hath filled the hungry with good things; and the rich he hath sent empty away. He hath holpen [helped] his servant Israel, in remembrance of his mercy; As he spake to our fathers, to Abraham, and to his seed for ever" (vv. 50–55).

¶ Luke 1:56
Mary stays until John is born.

The scripture records that "Mary abode with her about three months, and returned to her own house." That would have been the last three months of Elisabeth's pregnancy, since she arrived when Elisabeth was in her sixth month. And since this was in Mary's third month of pregnancy, it follows that John the Baptist was born just six months earlier than Jesus.

The Difficulties at Bethlehem

¶ Luke 2:4–5
Joseph takes his pregnant wife Mary to Bethlehem.

They resided at the time in Nazareth, a city of Galilee, but "because he was of the house and lineage of David" they were required to travel "into Judæa, unto the city of David, which is called Bethlehem" in order to be "taxed" [counted in the census] (vv. 4–5). Mary was "great with child" (v. 5)—in her ninth month of pregnancy—when they left their home in Nazareth and traveled (probably riding donkeys) a distance of from 80 to 90 miles to Bethlehem.

¶ Luke 2:6
Mary is already in labor when they arrive at Bethlehem,

So Joseph sought earnestly for a comfortable setting for the birth of their baby. He hoped to find room in one of the inns surrounding Bethlehem square.

¶ Luke 2:7
Nobody made room for Mary in the inns.

Because Mary's condition probably required slow travel, when they arrived all of the inns were already full. And because of the crowded conditions and the insensitivity that often exists in crowded masses of people, "there was none to give room for them in the inns" (JST, Luke 2:7). Note that there was no innkeeper. This is a quaint notion that arises out of the English translation of an "inn" as a sort of hotel with beds.

J. AUBERT, THE BIBLE AND ITS STORY, 1908,

Joseph seeks shelter in vain for his pregnant wife

Inns were square buildings, open on one side, which faced the city square, and in which travelers commonly put up for the night.

These *khans* or *caravanseries* were not much more than crudely constructed roofs over open public courts. Frederic Farrar said: "[They were] perfectly public; everything that takes place in them is visible to every person in the khan [and] totally devoid of even the most ordinary furniture."[10]

Elder Bruce R. McConkie said: "Though her state was apparent, the other travelers—lacking in courtesy, compassion, and refinement—would not give way so she could be cared for. . . . It was the traveling hosts of Judah . . . not just an innkeeper or an isolated few persons . . . who withheld shelter from Joseph and Mary. . . . This rude rejection was but prelude to the coming day when these same people and their children after them would reject to their eternal sorrow the Lord who that night began mortality under the most lowly circumstances."[11]

The Savior's Humble Birth

¶ Luke 2:7
The Christ child is born in a filthy stable.

Joseph and Mary had to settle for whatever shelter they could find in the stables. Livestock stalls were attached to the outside or back of the inns, and the innermost part of these stalls (or nearby caves were used as stables. It was the only place offering a roof overhead and reasonable privacy for the imminent birth of their baby. As we imagine those circumstances, we can smell the smells and hear the flies that cattle stalls attract. We can imagine Joseph gathering hay and spreading it upon the filthy floor to make Mary more comfortable and the birth more sanitary.

And then there, alone and inexperienced, exhausted, in pain from labor, hurt by the rejection of others, and probably frightened, Mary lay down in a filthy cattle stall and, with Joseph's help, delivered her precious little baby boy.

Notes

1. *The Mortal Messiah: From Bethlehem to Calvary*, 4 vols. (1979–81), 1:326–27, note 4.
2. *Doctrinal New Testament Commentary*, 3 vols. (1965–73), 1:85.
3. See *History of the Church*, 3:386.
4. *The Mortal Messiah: From Bethlehem to Calvary*, 1:318–19.
5. *Doctrinal New Testament Commentary*, 1:82–83.
6. *A Companion to Your Study of the New Testament: The Four Gospels* (1982), 27.
7. *The Promised Messiah: The First Coming of Christ* (1978), 470–71.
8. *Jesus the Christ*, 3rd ed. (1916), 81.
9. *Doctrinal New Testament Commentary*, 1:84–85.
10. *The Life of Christ* (1874), 33.
11. *Doctrinal New Testament Commentary*, 1:92.

Chapter 5

Annunciation in America

(Helaman 14; 3 Nephi 1)

ℌℭ

The momentous birth of the Savior occurred in the land of Judah. But at least one other group of people was fully aware of its happening. Halfway around the world, humble believers prayed mightily for His coming and looked for the signs of His birth. Then finally, on the night before His immortal spirit entered His earthly tabernacle, the Lord's Spirit appeared to the prophet Nephi and declared, "Behold, the time is at hand, and on this night shall the sign be given, and on the morrow come I into the world" (3 Nephi 1:13).

The Nephites were watching for the signs prophesied by Samuel the Lamanite five years earlier. This great prophet in the Western Hemisphere had predicted with accuracy many signs of the Savior's birth and also His death.

Samuel the Lamanite

Samuel's message was rejected by the Nephites, who were extremely wicked at the time. They cast him out of the city of Zarahemla, but he returned to deliver a stirring warning of destruction if they did not repent. His prophecies covered not only that present time, but also their future destruction 400 years later (see Helaman chapters 13–15). To deliver his message, he stood upon a wall while spears and rocks were thrown at him. The Lord protected him until he had finished his message; then he disappeared into the wilderness, never to be heard from again. It was during these stirring events that Samuel issued his prophecies concerning Christ.

Signs of the Coming of Christ

¶ Helaman 14:2–7
Signs of the birth of Jesus Christ.

The Nephites were watching for the signs prophesied by Samuel the Lamanite five years earlier. This great prophet predicted with remarkable accuracy many signs of the Savior's birth and also His death.

The fact that Samuel delivered these prophesies while standing upon a wall with rocks and arrows flying all around him makes them all the more impressive.

Samuel the Lamanite's prophecy:	The Fulfillment:
— Christ to be born in five years (v. 2)	3 Nephi 1:13
— No darkness for "one day and a night and a day" (vv. 3–4)	3 Nephi 1:15
— "A new star [to] arise" (v. 5)	3 Nephi 1:21
— "Many signs and wonders in heaven" (v. 6)	3 Nephi 1:19–22
— People to "fall to the earth" (v. 7)	3 Nephi 1:16–18

The Importance of Christ's Birth

¶ Helaman 14:12
Samuel quotes King Benjamin.

This is a precise repetition of Benjamin's key words in Mosiah 3:8. This is remarkable since this part of the Book of Mormon was translated much later than the Book of Mosiah. Joseph Smith had no access to the earlier script at the time he dictated these words. It is yet another internal evidence of the authenticity of the Book of Mormon.

King Benjamin (Mosiah 3:8)	Samuel the Lamanite (Hel. 14:12)
And he shall be called	And also that ye might know of the coming of
Jesus Christ, the Son of God, the Father of heaven and earth, the Creator of all things from the beginning;	Jesus Christ, the Son of God, the Father of heaven and of earth, the Creator of all things from the beginning;
and his mother shall be called Mary.	and that ye might know of the signs of his coming, to the intent that ye might believe on his name.

¶ Helaman 14:12

Names and titles of the Savior.

Who was the babe born in Bethlehem? This scripture establishes without question His deity. He is called "Jesus Christ, the Son of God, the Father of heaven and of earth, [and] the Creator of all things from the beginning." His role as Creator makes Him the "Father" of all things created on this earth, including our own bodies. And as the "Creator of all things from the beginning," we understand that all things throughout the universe were likewise created by Him.

¶ Helaman 14:13

We may receive a remission of our sins through the "merits" of Christ.

Merits are qualities or actions that entitle a person to claim rewards. This analogy works well to explain the connection between the suffering of Christ and the sanctification that we must obtain in order to dwell with our Father in the celestial kingdom. We are not capable of living without sin in this fallen world. But if we do "all we can do" (2 Nephi 25:23), then through repentance and faith, and by virtue of the "merits" of Christ's Atonement, we can be "made clean" despite our failings.

— 2 Nephi 2:7–9

> It is only through the Savior's merits that we can be forgiven of sins. Lehi taught his son Jacob that Christ "offereth himself a sacrifice for sin, to answer the ends of the law, unto all those who have a broken heart and a contrite spirit; and unto none else can the ends of the law be answered" (v. 7).

The Signs of Christ's Birth Appear

¶ 3 Nephi 1:4–9

The time predicted by Samuel for the birth of the Savior (5 years) arrives without the predicted sign, and the wicked threaten to kill all believers.

As the day of the Lord's birth approached "the prophecies of the prophets began to be fulfilled more fully; for there began to be greater signs and greater miracles wrought among the people" (v. 4). But the major signs that were to appear at His birth had not yet appeared.

Disbelievers said that the time had passed in which the prophecies of Samuel the Lamanite were supposed to be fulfilled (v. 5). This, of course, caused them to rejoice because they assumed that the believers' faith had been in vain (v. 6). They loudly proclaimed their view, to the great sorrow of believers who feared that maybe the prophecies would not be fulfilled (v. 7).

Nevertheless, believers continued to watch and pray for the sign—a "day and [a] night and [a] day which should be as one day as if there were no night" (v. 8). Meanwhile, disbelievers set a deadline for the sign to appear, after which they would put to death anybody who continued to believe in the prophecy of Samuel the Lamanite (v. 9).

THEBIBLEREVIVAL.COM, #23

Believers continued to watch and pray for Christ's coming

¶ 3 Nephi 1:10–14

Nephi prays for his people and the Lord declares, "On the morrow come I into the world."

Nephi, the son of Nephi, newly ordained to his prophetic office became "exceedingly sorrowful" over the wickedness of the people (v. 10). He humbly bowed himself to the earth and "cried mightily to his God in behalf of his people," meaning those who "were about to be destroyed because of their faith" (v. 11).

THEBIBLEREVIVAL.COM, #22

Nephi prayed mightily in behalf of his people

After praying mightily all day, the voice of the Lord spoke to him (v. 12), saying, "Lift up your head and be of good cheer; for behold, the time is at hand, and on this night shall the sign be given, and on the morrow come I into the world, to show unto the world that I will fulfil all that which I have caused to be spoken by the mouth of my holy prophets" (v. 13). We can only imagine the joy Nephi must have felt, not only that his people would be spared but that the Son of God would now "come unto [His]own, to fulfil all things which [He has] made known unto the children of men from the foundation of the world" (v. 14).

¶ 3 Nephi 1:15–23

All of the signs of the Savior's birth appear.

There was a day and a night and a day without darkness, causing great astonishment among the people (v. 15). Many of those who had not believed Samuel's prophecy "fell to the earth and became as if they were dead" because they knew that their plan to destroy the believers had failed (v. 16) and they knew "that the Son of God must shortly appear" (v. 17). In fact, the astonishment was so widespread that the Book of Mormon declares "all the people upon the face of the whole earth from the west to the east, both in the land north and in the land south, were so exceedingly astonished that they fell to the earth" (v. 17), fearing "because of their iniquity and their unbelief" (v. 18).

The next morning the sun rose as usual, indicating that a new day had arrived, "and they knew that it was the day that the Lord should be born, because of the sign which had been given" (v. 19). Then, one by one, all of the other predictions came to pass, including the appearance of a "new star" (vv. 20–21). The hard of heart continued to disbelieve, spreading lies about the signs that had appeared, but the "more part of the people" were "converted unto the Lord" (v. 22). Nephi and other priesthood holders "went forth among the people . . . baptizing unto repentance [and] remission of sins" and establishing peace in the land once again (v. 23).

— **Zechariah 14:7**

These same signs will appear at Christ's Second Coming.

The signs that appeared at Christ's birth will be shown again to the world just prior to His Second Coming, including a night in which there will be no darkness (Zechariah 14:7).

J. MARTIN

When night came, there was no darkness

AMBROGIO LORENZETTI, 1319

Jesus was wrapped in swaddling clothes

Chapter 6

The Birth and Childhood of Jesus

(Luke 2; Matthew 2)

ജ്ഗ

Do we fully appreciate "the condescension of God" in lowering Himself into such a humble birth? Cattle stalls are filthy, smelly, insect-harboring and crowded places. Yet, in such a filthy stall, the Savior of mankind and Creator of the visible universe was born.

He came into the world as we all do—helpless, dependent, and subject to sickness and pain. As Isaiah said: "He shall grow up . . . as a tender plant, and as a root out of a dry ground: he hath no form nor comeliness; and when we shall see him, there is no beauty that we should desire him" (Isaiah 53:2). In other words, He looked like any other baby and had the same needs.

¶ Luke 2:7
Jesus was wrapped in swaddling clothes.

"Swaddling clothes consisted of a cloth tied together by bandage-like strips. After an infant was born, the umbilical cord was cut and tied, and then the baby was washed, rubbed with salt and oil, and wrapped with strips of cloth. These strips kept the newborn child warm and also ensured that the child's limbs would grow straight."[1]

Anciently, it was believed that wrapping infants snugly in swaddling cloths or blankets, so that movement of the limbs was tightly restricted, was essential to helping infants develop proper posture. Even today, medical studies say that it helps babies to sleep and remain asleep. It also lowers the possibility of sudden infant death syndrome (SIDS).

Mary laid the Christ child in a manger

¶ Luke 2:7
Laid in a manger.

There was no bed or bassinet in which to lay Him. The floor would be too cold and hard. So Mary chose a straw-filled manger, usually used for feeding the cattle, as the resting place for her newborn baby. We have no idea how long the family stayed in the stable, but it was probably until the census was over and the crowds dispersed. It was there in the stable that the shepherds adored Him. So the manger was His bed for more than one night and possibly for quite a while.

RAPHAEL, 1509–10

Mary, Joseph, and their new baby

"Tonight You Are Mine"

We can imagine the fear of these new parents—and also their joy. We are touched by the story of a newborn child coming into the world. We reflect on our own first experiences with our own children, holding and kissing them with feelings of pure joy. That was also the situation for Joseph and Mary, and the beauty of the story never fades, no matter how many times it is told.

When I picture this tender family scene, I am reminded of a beautiful carol called "Mary's Lullaby (Tonight You Are Mine)," written by Wanda West Palmer,[2] which relates what may have been Mary's feelings on that occasion. She knew that this child was coming into the world to save it. All sorts of trials and abuses lay ahead, culminating in the brutal and bloody suffering and death of her Son. But on that night—that sacred holy night—He was their helpless little baby.

Let us imagine those first quiet moments. Mary and Joseph must have caressed those little hands and feet. Did they know what soldiers would eventually do to those hands and feet? They must have kissed His little cheeks—the same cheeks that priests would rudely slap, and from which the hair of His beard would be pulled by the handful. They must have gently bathed His tiny back, side, and belly—a back that would one day be ripped by vicious scourges, a belly that would heave with pain on the cross, and a side that would be pierced with a deep, sharp spear.

Did they know all these things on that night? Maybe and maybe not. But at that moment He was simply their miraculous little child, and they certainly must have rejoiced over His birth.

The Heavenly Host of Angels

¶ Luke 2:8–14
"Unto you is born this day . . . a Saviour, which is Christ the Lord."

On the night of the Savior's birth, there were shepherds in the nearby fields of Bethlehem (v. 8). Suddenly, an "angel of the Lord" appeared unto them, causing his glorified light to shine all around them (v. 9). Understandably, "they were sore afraid," but the angel sought to calm their fears: "Fear not: for, behold, I bring you good tidings of great joy, which shall be to all people. For unto you is born this day in the city of David a Saviour, which is Christ the Lord" (vv. 10–11).

Suddenly, there appeared with the angel "a multitude of the heavenly host praising God" by singing "glory to God in the highest, and on earth peace, good will toward men" (vv. 13–14). We can imagine that every child of God still then in heaven might have wished to sing on this occasion. After all, the salvation of all humankind would now be made possible. This precious baby was born to save us all. As the Lamb of God, He would be sacrificed for our sins. He was born to die so that all of us might have redemption and resurrection. This was great news, joyful news indeed. The Hope of Israel had come!

The Shepherds

¶ Luke 2:12,15–17
The shepherds "made known abroad . . . concerning this child."

The angel had given them a sign: "Ye shall find the babe wrapped in swaddling clothes, lying in a manger" (v. 12). Thus, as soon as the angels left them, "the shepherds said one to another, Let us now go even unto Bethlehem, and see this thing which is come to pass, which the Lord hath made known unto us. And they came with haste, and found Mary, and Joseph, and the babe lying in a manger" (vv. 15–16). And having seen it for themselves, "they made known abroad the saying which was told them concerning this child" (v. 17).

Elder Bruce R. McConkie said: "These were not ordinary shepherds nor ordinary flocks. The sheep there being . . . cared for with love and devotion—were destined for sacrifice on the great altar in the Lord's House, in similitude of the eternal sacrifice of Him who that wondrous night lay in a stable. . . . And the shepherds—for whom the veil was then rent . . . were [of] spiritual stature. . . . There were many shepherds in Palestine, but only to those who watched over the temple flocks did the herald angel come; only they heard the heavenly choir."[3]

C. H. BLOCH, 1600s

The adoration of the shepherds

Simeon in the Temple

¶ Luke 2:22–24
Jesus is dedicated to the Lord's service at 40 days old.

Just as Zacharias and Elisabeth had done for John the Baptist (Luke 1:59), Mary and Joseph no doubt had Jesus circumcised when He became eight days old. But this additional dedication ceremony, about one month later, was required for all firstborn males, who were considered "holy to the Lord" (v. 23). It was accompanied by a sacrifice of two turtledoves, or two young pigeons (v. 24).

Elder James E. Talmage said:

> Part of the law given through Moses to the Israelites in the wilderness and continued in force down through the centuries, related to the procedure prescribed for women after childbirth (Leviticus 12). In compliance therewith, Mary remained in retirement forty days following the birth of her Son; then she and her husband brought the Boy for presentation before the Lord as prescribed for the male firstborn of every family.
>
> It is manifestly impossible that all such presentations could have taken place in the temple, for many Jews lived at great distances from Jerusalem; it was the rule, however, that parents should present their children in the temple when possible. Jesus was born within five or six miles from Jerusalem; He was accordingly taken to the temple for the ceremonial of redemption from the requirement applying to the firstborn of all Israelites except Levites.[4]

F. W. W. TOPHAM, 1889

¶ Luke 2:25–33

Simeon testifies that this is the Christ.

There was a man in Jerusalem named Simeon who the Bible describes as "just and devout, waiting for the consolation of Israel: and the Holy Ghost was upon him" (v. 25). It had been promised to him "that he should not see death, before he had seen the Lord's Christ" (v. 26), and on this particular day "he came by the Spirit into the temple" (v. 27).

He discerned by the Spirit who the child was, and "took . . . him up in his arms, and blessed God, and said, Lord, now lettest thou thy servant depart in peace, according to thy word: For mine eyes have seen thy salvation, which thou hast prepared before the face of all people" (vv. 28–31). He went on to testify that the child would be "a light to . . . the Gentiles, and the glory of thy people Israel" (v. 32).

THEBIBLEREVIVAL.COM, #26

¶ Luke 2:34–35

Simeon's prophecy of the Savior's death and Mary's sorrow.

He told Mary, "Behold, this child is set for the fall and rising again of many in Israel; and for a sign which shall be spoken against . . . that the thoughts of many hearts may be revealed." And as part of that process, he said to Mary, "a sword shall pierce through thy own soul also" (v. 35). Elder James E. Talmage said that this prophecy was of "the anguish that the mother would be called to endure because of Him, which would be even like unto that of a sword piercing her soul."[5]

Anna in the Temple

¶ Luke 2:36–38, 41
Anna also bears witness.

This woman, after seven years of marriage, had endured widowhood until the age of 84. She also came in at that instant and "gave thanks likewise unto the Lord, and spake of him to all them that looked for redemption in Jerusalem" (v. 38).

Elder James E. Talmage called her "a godly woman of great age, . . . who devoted herself exclusively to temple service; and she, being inspired of God, recognized her Redeemer, and testified of Him to all about her. Both Joseph and Mary marveled at the things that were spoken of the Child; seemingly they were not yet able to comprehend the majesty of Him who had come to them through so miraculous a conception and so marvelous a birth."[6]

The Wise Men from the East

¶ Matthew 2:1–2
"We have seen his star in the east, and are come to worship him."

Some time later, "there came wise men from the east to Jerusalem," who had "seen his star in the east, and [had] come to worship him." We do not know where they came from, but it is possible that they came from Persia, where a large colony of Jews had remained since the captivity.

GUSTAVE DORÉ, 1896

Wise men came from the east

Daniel H. Ludlow said: "The statement of the wise men 'We have seen his star in the east' is extremely interesting inasmuch as the star as a sign at the birth of Jesus is not mentioned in the present Old Testament. However, reference to the sign of a star was mentioned by Samuel the Lamanite in the Book of Mormon some five years before the birth of Jesus (Helaman 14:1–5; 3 Nephi 1:21). The . . . language used by the wise men would indicate that other groups besides the Lehites were aware that a new star would bear record of the birth of the Son of God [but] 'attempts have been made to identify the star whose appearance in their eastern sky had assured the magi that the King was born; but astronomy furnishes no satisfactory confirmation.'"[7]

Elder Bruce R. McConkie said: "As to the star, there is nothing mysterious about it. The Magi . . . were not reading portents in the skies nor divining the destinies of men by the movement of celestial bodies in the sidereal heavens. The new star was simply a new star of the sort we are familiar with. No doubt it exhibited an unusual brilliance, so as to attract special attention and so as to give guidance to those who walked in its light, but it was, nonetheless, a star."[8]

The Prophet Joseph Smith said (speaking of Christ's Second Coming): "There will be wars and rumors of wars, signs in the heavens above and on the earth beneath, the sun turned into darkness and the moon to blood, earthquakes in divers places, the seas heaving beyond their bounds; then will appear one grand sign of the Son of Man in heaven. But what will the world do? They will say it is a planet, a comet, etc. But the Son of Man will come as the sign of the coming of the Son of Man, which will be as the light of the morning cometh out of the east."[9]

¶ Matthew 2:1–10
"Where is he that is born King of the Jews?"

When the eastern wise men arrived in the city they asked where the new king had been born. When Herod heard the child described as the "King of the Jews," he "was troubled, and all Jerusalem with him" (v. 3). He called together all of the Jewish chief priests and scribes and "demanded of them where Christ should be born" (v. 4). They answered "in Bethlehem of Judæa: for thus it is written by the prophet," quoting Micah 5:2.

Herod then "called the wise men [to him, and] inquired of them diligently what time the star appeared" (v. 7). Then he sent them to Bethlehem with a request that "when ye have found him, bring me word again, that I may come and worship him also" (v. 8). "They departed; and, lo, the star, which they saw in the east, went before them, till it came and stood over where the young child was" and "when they saw the star, they rejoiced with exceeding great joy" (vv. 9–10).

¶ Matthew 2:11
The wise men visit Jesus in a house, not a stable.

By the time the wise men had arrived, Joseph, Mary, and the baby were no longer in the stable. The scriptures say specifically that they "were come into the house" (v. 11). Also, the child was no longer a newborn, but is described as a "young child" (v. 11).

Elder Bruce R. McConkie said: "The wise men found Jesus in a house, not a stable, inn, or temporary abiding place; that He is called a 'young child,' not a baby, a total of seven times in the course of 14 consecutive verses [and] that Matthew makes two pointed references to the diligent nature of Herod's inquiry as to the actual time of the birth, . . . assuming that Herod would order the massacre of all young children in the general age bracket, . . . the presumption arises that a number of months or even one or two years may have elapsed before the arrival of the eastern visitors."[10]

¶ Matthew 2:11
The wise men present the child with gifts.

They "fell down, and worshipped him: and when they had opened their treasures, they presented unto him gifts; gold, and frankincense, and myrrh."

Elder James E. Talmage said: "The tendency to ascribe occult significance to even trifling details mentioned in scripture . . . has led to many fanciful suggestions concerning the gold and frankincense and myrrh specified in this incident. Some have supposed a half-hidden symbolism therein—gold a tribute to His royal estate, frankincense an offering in recognition of His priesthood, and myrrh for His burial. The sacred record offers no basis for such conjecture. . . . They were presumably among the natural productions of the lands from which the magi came, though

RUBENS, 1626–1629

probably even there they were costly and highly esteemed. Such . . . were most appropriate as gifts for a king. Any mystical significance one may choose to attach to the presents must be remembered as his own supposition or fancy, and not as based on scriptural warrant."[11]

Jesus and John the Baptist Are Protected

King Herod did not intend to allow a rival king to survive. He had carefully determined where the child would be born and when the star announcing His birth appeared (Matthew 2:4–7). He was plotting to assassinate the Christ child.

¶ Matthew 2:12
The wise men are warned to avoid Herod.

This warning, given in a dream, said "that they should not return to Herod." Had they done so, he would have demanded to know where the child could be found. Instead, "they departed into their own country another way."

Joseph Takes Jesus into Egypt

¶ Matthew 2:13–15
Joseph and Mary flee into Egypt with the baby.

An angel of the Lord "appear[ed] to Joseph in a dream, saying, Arise, and take the young child and his mother, and flee into Egypt, and be thou there until I bring thee word: for Herod will seek the young child to destroy him" (v. 13). And "when he arose, he took the young child and his mother by night, and departed into Egypt" (v. 14), where the young family remained "until the death of Herod" (v. 15).

We discussed the holy family's sojourn in Egypt as part of Joseph's story in chapter 2. During their absence, Herod slaughtered all male children in Bethlehem under the age of two. It was not until the death of Herod that Jesus and His parents were able to safely return to their homeland.

Jesus's Childhood and Youth

The scriptures about Jesus's childhood are few and far between. But from the ones that do exist, a picture emerges of an extraordinary boy raised in a typical Jewish household.

— **Isaiah 53:2**

He grew up "[like] a tender plant" and looked like other children.

A. BIDA, 1874

— **D&C 93:12–14**

He did not have a fulness of godhood or knowledge at first, but continued from "grace to grace" until He received a fulness.

— **Luke 2:51–52**

He lived with His parents in Nazareth and was obedient to them.

— **Mark 6:3**

He was called a carpenter, showing that He learned a trade, probably under Joseph's direction.

— **Luke 2:40, 52**

He grew in all of these aspects.

- Spirit — Spiritually.
- Wisdom — Intellectually.
- Grace — Divine help.
- Stature — Physical growth.
- Favor with God — Pleasing His Heavenly Father.
- Favor with man — Social growth.

He Learned "Line upon Line," Just as We Do

¶ Jesus had a veil of forgetfulness regarding premortal life—like all of us.

Elder James E. Talmage said: "[When Jesus was born,] the veil of forgetfulness common to all who are born to earth, by which the remembrance of primeval existence is shut off [was cast over Him]."[12] "[But even as a child] He had all the intelligence necessary to enable Him to . . . govern the kingdom of the Jews"[13] because He overcame the veil and came into communication with His Heavenly Father.

President Joseph F. Smith said: "Even Christ Himself was not perfect [in knowledge or understanding] at first; He received not a fulness at first, but He received grace for grace, and He continued to receive more and more until He received a fulness. . . . Jesus, the Son of God, and the Father of the heavens and the earth in which we dwell, received not a fulness at the first, but increased in faith, knowledge, understanding, and grace until He received a fulness."[14]

President Joseph Fielding Smith said:

> Our Savior was a God before He was born into this world, and He brought with Him that same status when He came here. He was as much a God when He was born into the world as He was before. But as far as this life is concerned it appears that He had to start just as all other children do and gain His knowledge line upon line. . . .
>
> Without doubt, Jesus came into the world subject to the same condition as was required of each of us—He forgot everything, and He had to grow from grace to grace. His forgetting, or having His former knowledge taken away, would be requisite just as it is in the case of each of us, to complete the present temporal existence.[15]

He Was Taught by His Father in Heaven

¶ Luke 2:41–47
At age 12, Jesus converses with learned doctors in the temple.

His parents traveled to Jerusalem every year for the feast of the Passover (v. 41). On Jesus's twelfth birthday, they were there as always, returning home after the end of the required days of celebration and worship (v. 41).

They traveled a day's journey along the road and did not realize Jesus was not with them until they prepared to settle down for the night; He could not be found anywhere among His friends and family (vv. 42–44). Alarmed, they hurried back to Jerusalem and searched for three days. Then, finally, they "found him in the temple, sitting in the midst of the doctors" (v. 46). Having been taught by His Father in Heaven, His training and intelligence showed as He talked with these learned men in the temple, "both hearing them, and asking them questions" (v. 46). "And all that heard him were astonished at his understanding and answers" (v. 47).

W. H. HUNT, 1860

Mary finds Jesus in the temple with the doctors

Elder Bruce R. McConkie said:

> Under Jewish law, Jesus, now twelve, became "a son of the law"—one subject to its obligations. Now He rated a position in the congregation and stood forth as a recognized member of His home community. His religious and secular studies entered an advanced stage; His vocational preparations were intensified; and He could no longer be sold by His parents as a bond-servant.
>
> That He should now be taken to the annual Passover celebration was a natural and expected thing; and that He should enter the temple courts, join the discussion groups, listen to the expositions of the rabbis, and ask and answer questions Himself, was in perfect keeping with the customs of the day. The significance of His youthful appearance in the temple lies, not in the fact of its occurrence, but in the divine wisdom manifest by Him in His conversation and in the testimony which He then bore of His own divinity.[16]

¶ Luke 2:48–50

Jesus wants to be doing "[His] Father's business."

Mary gently chided Jesus by saying, "Son, why hast thou thus dealt with us? behold, thy father and I have sought thee sorrowing" (v. 48). Fully aware of His calling and His relationship to His Father in Heaven, Jesus asked, "How is it that ye sought me? wist ye not that I must be about my Father's business?" (v. 49). In the pressure of the moment, "they understood not the saying which he spake unto them" (v. 50), but from our later vantage point we can see that He was reminding her of just who His Father was and why He had sent Him to earth.

¶ John 8:28

He was instructed directly by our Father in Heaven, and had His guidance continually.

To the Jews He said: "I do nothing of myself; but as my Father hath taught me, I speak these things."

President Joseph Fielding Smith said: "[By the time] He was 12 years old . . . He astonished the doctors and wise men in the temple—He had learned a great deal about His Father's business. This knowledge could come to Him by revelation, by the visitation of angels, or in some other way. But His knowledge, so far as this life was concerned, had to come line upon line and precept upon precept. Without question He was in communication, from time to time, with His Heavenly Father."[17]

¶ John 12:49

He spoke only those things the Father told Him to speak.

"I have not spoken of myself," He declared, "but the Father which sent me, he gave me a commandment, what I should say, and what I should speak." No doubt He also attended the Jewish synagogue schools and was taught in the learning of the Jews by the rabbis.

HEINRICH HOFMANN, 1882

¶ JST, Matthew 3:24–25

He served under Joseph, but "he needed not that any man should teach him."

The JST says that "Jesus grew up with his brethren, and waxed strong, and waited upon the Lord for the time of his ministry to come" (v. 24). He obediently "served under his father [Joseph]," but He "spake not as other men, neither could he be taught; for he needed not that any man should teach him" (v. 25). (Compare with the limited information provided in Matthew 2:23 and Luke 2:40, 52.)

The Prophet Joseph Smith said: "When still a boy, He had all the intelligence necessary to enable Him to rule and govern the kingdom of the Jews, and could reason with the wisest and most profound doctors of law and divinity, and make their theories and practice to appear like folly compared with the wisdom He possessed; but He was a boy only, and lacked physical strength even to defend His own person; and was subject to cold, to hunger, and to death."[18]

¶ JST, Matthew 3:26

Jesus grows into manhood.

The normal age at which a young rabbi might begin his mission was 30. Jesus waited until that age to begin His ministry. Until that time, He spent His days in Nazareth, learning Joseph's trade as a carpenter and in every other way preparing Himself for what was to come. And then, "after many years, the hour of his ministry drew nigh."

We can imagine Him closing up His shop for the last time, laying aside the

Jesus bids his mother Mary goodbye

tools, and saying thank you and goodbye to Joseph and His mother Mary. He was now set to begin the mission for which He had been sent to earth—teaching, healing, blessing, and raising from the dead, followed by His infinite atonement, death, resurrection, and ascension. All this would be accomplished in the short span of three years.

Notes

1. Bromiley, *The International Standard Bible Encyclopedia*, reprint, rev. ed. (1995), "Swaddling."
2. Jackman Music Corporation, JK.00479.
3. *The Mortal Messiah: From Bethlehem to Calvary*, 4 vols. (1979–81), 1:347.
4. *Jesus the Christ*, 3rd ed. (1916), 95.
5. *Jesus the Christ*, 97.
6. *Jesus the Christ*, 97.
7. *A Companion to Your Study of the New Testament: The Four Gospels* (1982), 29. Also, James E. Talmage, in *Jesus the Christ*, 3rd ed. (1916), 99, is quoted herein.
8. *The Mortal Messiah*, 1:359.
9. *Teachings of Presidents of the Church: Joseph Smith* (2007), 252–53.
10. *Doctrinal New Testament Commentary*, 3 vols. (1965–73), 1:107.
11. *Jesus the Christ*, 108, note 4.
12. *Jesus the Christ*, 111.
13. *Teachings of Presidents of the Church: Joseph Smith* (2007), 53.
14. *Gospel Doctrine*, 5th ed. (1939), 68.
15. *Doctrines of Salvation*, comp. Bruce R. McConkie, 3 vols. (1954–56), 1:32, 33.
16. *Doctrinal New Testament Commentary*, 1:109–10.
17. *Doctrines of Salvation*, 1:32.
18. *History of the Church*, 6:608.

About the Author

Randal S. Chase spent his childhood years in Nephi, Utah, where his father was a dry land wheat farmer and a businessman. In 1959 their family moved to Salt Lake City and settled in the Holladay area. He served a full-time mission in the Central British (England Central) Mission from 1968 to 1970. He returned home and married Deborah Johnsen in 1971. They are the parents of six children—two daughters and four sons—and an ever-expanding number of grandchildren.

He was called to serve as a bishop at the age of 27 in the Sandy Crescent South Stake area of the Salt Lake Valley. He served six years in that capacity, and has since served as a high councilor, a stake executive secretary and clerk, and in many other stake and ward callings. Regardless of whatever other callings he has received over the years, one was nearly constant: He has taught Gospel Doctrine classes in every ward he has ever lived in as an adult—a total of 35 years.

Dr. Chase was a well-known media personality on Salt Lake City radio stations in the 1970s. He left on-air broadcasting in 1978 to develop and market a computer-based management, sales, and music programming system to radio and television stations in the United States, Canada, South America, and Australia. After the business was sold in 1984, he supported his family as a media and business consultant in the Salt Lake City area.

Having a great desire to teach young people of college age, he determined in the late 1980s to pursue his doctorate, and received his PhD in Communication from the University of Utah in 1997. He has taught communication courses at that institution as well as at Salt Lake Community College and Dixie State University for 21 years. He is currently a Professor and full-time faculty member, and former Department Chair, in the Communication Department at Dixie State University in St. George, Utah.

Concurrently with his academic career, Brother Chase has served as a volunteer LDS Institute and Adult Education instructor in the CES system since 1994, both in Salt Lake City and St. George, where he currently teaches a weekly Adult Education class for three stakes in the Washington area. He has also conducted multiple Church History tours and seminars.

During these years of gospel teaching, he has developed an extensive library of lesson plans and handouts which are the predecessors to his 13-volume series of study guides titled *Making Precious Things Plain*, and several other books on Gospel topics. They are designed to assist teachers and students of Gospel Doctrine classes, as well as those who simply want to study on their own, our wonderful scriptural legacy of faith and revelation during every dispensation of the earth.

CPSIA information can be obtained
at www.ICGtesting.com
Printed in the USA
JSHW021343201219
3092JS00004B/32